34
T. C. 12.

RÉSUMÉ

DE

PLUSIEURS CONSIDÉRATIONS ET PROJETS

Tendant à la conservation des militaires et à l'économie dans les dépenses des Départemens de la Guerre, de la Marine, de l'Intérieur et de l'Instruction publique.

PAR B. L. PEYRE,

Chevalier de l'ordre royal de la Légion-d'Honneur, Docteur en médecine, Chirurgien-Major du dix-huitième régiment d'infanterie de ligne.

PARIS,

IMPRIMERIE DE H. FOURNIER,

RUE DE SEINE, N° 14.

Avril 1828.

RÉSUMÉ

DE

PLUSIEURS CONSIDÉRATIONS ET PROJETS.

CHAPITRE PREMIER.

Instruction à donner à Messieurs les Élèves des écoles militaires.

Dans les écoles de cavalerie on enseigne à Messieurs les Élèves l'hygiène pour la conservation des chevaux ; on a senti l'importance de ces connaissances, par lesquelles on peut prévenir beaucoup de maladies chez ces animaux. Eh ! l'on n'a pas encore pensé à enseigner aux Officiers l'hygiène de l'homme !!!... Ce contraste, bien surprenant et dont je ne puis me rendre raison, suffit pour démontrer l'indispensable nécessité de créer, dans chaque école militaire, un *Cours d'hygiène appliquée à la conservation des troupes.*

Riches de ces connaissances, les officiers pourraient indiquer aux soldats, dans chaque nouvelle position, dans chaque changement sur la manière d'être, ce qui peut le plus convenir ou suppléer au besoin et ce qu'il faut éviter de faire.

Cette instruction, facile à acquérir, qu'on peut donner à peu de frais, est d'autant plus utile que souvent en campagne, comme en temps de paix, les régimens sont détachés par compagnies qui manquent de Docteurs.

Il résulterait donc de cette éducation hygiénique un moins grand nombre de malades, avantage économique d'abord et bien grand en campagne où l'on ne saurait trop conserver le nombre de combattans, où l'encombrement des hôpitaux, toujours mal disposés, ajoute encore aux causes destructives de l'armée.

On peut regarder comme une vérité démontrée, que *la force morale, la bravoure, le courage, le noble sentiment de ses devoirs ne peuvent se rencontrer que chez l'homme sain; que ces vertus, indispensables pour être bon soldat, ne sauraient être le partage des hommes affaiblis par les maladies fréquentes* dont on pourrait, dans plus d'un cas, facilement les garantir.

Je ne puis mieux finir ce chapitre qu'en faisant des vœux pour que l'hygiène fasse partie de l'instruction qu'on donne dans tous les collèges : une partie de ces leçons serait un cours de morale très-persuasif puisqu'on démontrerait, par des faits, la funeste influence des passions sur la santé.

CHAPITRE II.

Étude médicale de l'Armée.

Pour être à même de connaître, par la suite, l'action de toutes les influences locales sur la santé des militaires, et de prononcer sur la salubrité ou sur l'insalubrité de chaque garnison et de chaque caserne; afin de savoir quel département produit les meilleurs soldats, au moral comme au physique, et les plus aptes au service de chaque arme, je propose qu'on exige de tous les Chirurgiens-Majors des corps, ce que je fais moi-même pour mon régiment : 1° de tenir un bulletin médical de chaque homme, pour inscrire successivement toutes les maladies dont chacun serait atteint; 2° de dresser des états sommaires, comparatifs, mensuels, trimestriels, semestriels et annuels du nombre de malades et de décès; 3° de noter le genre des pertes annuelles qu'éprouvent les contingens de chaque département, en faisant une étude médicale de ces hommes.

Un Chirurgien-principal, adjoint au Conseil de santé, près le Ministre de la guerre, ferait un résumé de tous les rapports qui lui seraient adressés et correspondrait, en outre, avec tous les Officiers de santé en chef des hôpitaux, pour réunir tous les faits se rapportant au travail dont il serait chargé, lequel travail serait très-étendu, au moins d'après le cadre que j'ai conçu.

Les travaux que je propose, et dont on ne peut contester la très-grande utilité, devant avoir pour résultat la conservation des militaires, en faisant remonter aux causes locales qui peuvent altérer leur santé, produiraient, par la suite, une économie considérable en hommes et en argent, puisqu'on serait plus à même de prévenir un grand nombre de maladies ainsi que leur suites fâcheuses.

La collection de tous les bulletins serait, dans quelques années, une source immense de matériaux, infiniment précieux, sous tous les rapports possibles, pour la science de l'homme.

CHAPITRE III

Voyage des recrues et des régimens.

Je prouve, par des faits incontestables, que l'état de dénuement dans lequel on fait voyager les jeunes soldats, en les mettant dans le cas de souffrir beaucoup des intempéries de la saison, les expose à devenir gravement malades et par suite à être promptement réformés ou à mourir sous peu de temps. Ce qui affaiblit considérablement l'armée, tout en occasionant de grandes dépenses, en pure perte.

Je propose pour obvier à ce triste état de choses : 1° d'habiller dans la tenue journalière les jeunes soldats, au jour de leur départ : ce qui n'augmenterait nullement les dépenses; car les effets, qu'on leur délivrerait, portés avec soin 20 ou 30 jours plus tôt, n'en feraient pas moins leur temps de durée déterminée; 2° de choisir la saison du printemps, de préférence, pour effectuer les voyages et les changemens de garnison; 3° de diviser la France géographiquement, comme le globe, en trois zones et de ne faire passer les recrues et les corps que d'une zone à l'autre, sans leur faire franchir la zone intermédiaire, afin d'éviter par là l'effet toujours sensible des trop grandes et trop brusques transitions.

Par les mesures que je propose, on aurait certainement bien moins de malades, de réformes et de décès, et naturellement plus de soldats à rendre à l'Agriculture et à l'Industrie.

CHAPITRE IV.

Moyens de garantir les militaires du froid et de l'humidité du pavé et de l'air pendant la nuit.

Je fais sentir combien l'action froide et humide du pavé des chambres, sur les pieds des soldats, et combien aussi le froid et l'humidité de l'air, peuvent influer sur la santé et l'altérer.

Pour soustraire les hommes à ces influences je propose : 1° de placer une planche mobile entre deux lits pour tenir lieu de parquet ; 2° de mettre dans chaque chambre une petite fosse inodore amovible, pour épargner aux soldats qui ont des besoins à satisfaire de sortir, de traverser les corridors et les cours comme ils sont obligés de le faire.

Je suis certain que si l'on employait les moyens que j'indique, on aurait bien moins de phlegmasies, de viscères thoraciques et abdominaux, qui sont les maladies dominantes dans les régimens, au moins dans les départemens du nord, lesquelles, passant très-facilement à l'état chronique, altèrent pour toujours la santé quand elles ne causent pas la mort. Ces maladies sont les principales causes des décès dans les hôpitaux militaires et les principaux motifs des congés de convalescence, d'un an et de réforme.

CHAPITRE V.

Utilisation du calorique qui se perd dans les cuisines des casernes.

Je fais pressentir une économie de la moitié du chauffage au moins, par un appareil que j'ai inventé, tout en ayant assez d'eau chaude pour pouvoir administrer, sans frais, un bain dans des cas urgens, qui se présentent assez souvent; pour faire baigner les malades qu'on traite à l'infirmerie et les hommes incorporés journellement, qui sont généralement très-malpropres;

enfin pour faire prendre des bains de propreté successivement à tous les hommes.

Par l'usage des bains, les maladies qui se déclarent subitement seraient souvent guéries ou perdraient certainement de leur intensité; celles qu'on traite à l'infirmerie guériraient plus vite et l'on en préviendrait beaucoup par plus de propreté.

Au moyen de mon appareil on pourrait administrer des bains de vapeur, et en dirigeant ces vapeurs dans les chambres on en élèverait de beaucoup la température dans les grands froids.

En employant le moyen caléfiant que je propose, on éviterait toujours les incendies causés par les cheminées en usage; sous ce dernier rapport cet appareil serait bien précieux pour la marine et pour tous les établissemens publics.

Pour la marine, la consommation moindre de bois ou de charbon, serait bien avantageuse, en favorisant le chargement productif des navires.

Quant aux établissemens publics, on aurait, par les feux de la cuisine et de la pharmacie, dans les hôpitaux, la faculté de supprimer le feu des bains, puisqu'on aurait toujours suffisamment d'eau chaude et l'on pourrait supprimer une partie des poêles dans les salles, car on pourrait en échauffer plusieurs par la vapeur.

Cet appareil durerait un grand nombre d'années ; une seule pièce, de la valeur d'à peu-près 100 fr., serait susceptible d'être changée au plus tous les deux ans ; un appareil-modèle, pouvant servir à faire la cuisine d'un bataillon, coûterait à peu-près 2,000 fr.

CHAPITRE VI.

Considérations sur les salles de police et les cachots.

Je signale l'insalubrité de ces lieux de détention par leur position au rez-de-chaussée et leur atmosphère froide et humide, qui devient encore plus délétère par la réunion d'un grand nombre d'hommes, et par les baquets qu'on leur laisse trop long-temps sans les vider.

Je fais ressortir l'inconvenance de mettre ensemble des hommes vicieux, qui, par leur réunion, se corrompent encore davantage : *les salles de police deviennent ainsi un enseignement mutuel du vice, où le coupable s'instruit à faire le mal, apprend à ne plus rougir, et d'où il ne peut sortir sans être encore plus pervers.*

Je propose, sous le rapport physique et moral, d'établir les salles de discipline dans les mansardes dont on ne fait ordinairement aucun usage, et de séparer les hommes punis chacun dans une loge : ce qui les punirait bien plus, et qui les garantirait d'une plus grande perversion.

CHAPITRE VII.

Considérations sur l'habillement et l'équipement.

En considérant la forme et la nature des objets qui habillent et arment le soldat, sous un point de vue hygiénique ou médical, je démontre qu'ils ne sont point assez en rapport avec les besoins des hommes qui en sont revêtus et armés ; je vois qu'on a tout sacrifié à l'agrément, tandis que cette considération est la dernière à laquelle il fallait avoir égard.

La simplicité doit être la parure d'un militaire, la propreté son élégance. A quoi servent les ornemens en diverses nuances, qui ne sont beaux qu'un jour, qui déparent l'uniforme quand ils sont fanés, et qu'on est souvent forcé de renouveler à grands frais? Que la tenue n'ait qu'une couleur dans chacune de ses parties, qu'elle ne soit point brillantée inutilement, celui qui la portera en aura plus de grâce; il pourra en outre l'entretenir propre plus facilement, et le Gouvernement y trouvera une grande économie.

Il me paraît aussi plus convenable de n'avoir qu'une seule tenue; car, par ce moyen, chaque homme aurait constamment un uniforme frais pour mettre les jours de fête et de parade : un régiment perd beaucoup, pour le coup d'œil, quand il paraît avec les habits qui en sont à leur troisième année de durée. Je conserverais la veste qui est très-convenable pour les travaux de l'intérieur, pour l'école des manœuvres, pour les corvées, et qui de plus peut être portée sous l'uniforme en hiver : c'est la seule partie de l'habillement sur laquelle il n'y ait rien à dire.

Je voudrais porter la réforme dans l'habillement jusqu'à n'avoir que la même tenue pour toutes les armes, en distinguant la cavalerie de l'infanterie par une partie de la coiffure, sauf à adopter des couleurs différentes pour chaque arme. Les militaires, ayant tous le même besoin d'être garantis des intempéries, devraient tous l'être par les mêmes moyens, c'est-à-dire également, au lieu de l'être plus ou moins comme ils le sont actuellement.

En démontrant que la tenue actuelle ne remplit point, ou ne remplit qu'imparfaitement les conditions indispensables de commodité, de simplicité, de légèreté et d'économie, c'est prouver que tout est à refaire. Dans cette idée, j'ai cherché à résoudre le problème suivant : *trouver une tenue qui ait le moins d'inconvéniens ou de défauts, et qui offre le plus d'avantages possible.* Je crois avoir trouvé la solution de ce problème ; car l'uniforme que j'ai imaginé garantirait mieux du froid, de la neige, de la pluie, sans tenir aucune partie du corps trop chaudement ; il serait plus aisé à mettre et à porter, plus simple, et bien moins dispendieux tant pour la confection que pour l'entretien.

En adoptant les modifications que je propose, l'équipement, réduit à une dépense très-minime, serait allégé du poids de 2 livres 14 onces pour les fusiliers, et de 3 livres 12 onces pour les sous-officiers, caporaux, grenadiers et voltigeurs : avantage bien grand dans les marches forcées, et lorsqu'il faut que les militaires se chargent de vivres pour plusieurs jours.

N. B Je préviens que je ne vendrai point l'appareil que j'ai inventé et que je propose. J'en dirigerai avec plaisir la confection, sans me charger d'autre chose.

www.ingramcontent.com/pod-product-compliance
Lightning Source LLC
Chambersburg PA
CBHW061627040426
42450CB00010B/2714

Too Short to Box with God

poems by

Matthew Johnson

Finishing Line Press
Georgetown, Kentucky

Too Short to Box with God

Copyright © 2024 by Matthew Johnson
ISBN 979-8-88838-652-1 First Edition
All rights reserved under International and Pan-American Copyright Conventions. No part of this book may be reproduced in any manner whatsoever without written permission from the publisher, except in the case of brief quotations embodied in critical articles and reviews.

ACKNOWLEDGMENTS

Grateful acknowledgment is made to the journals in which the following poems appeared, sometimes as different versions:

Across the Margin: "The Manassas Mauler on the Canvas"
Aethlon: Journal of Sports Literature: "Ordering Mike Tyson Fights on Pay-Per-View"
Jerry Jazz Musician: "Glimpse of Negro Pride in the Depression," "I Enjoy Little, Brown Clay," and "The Night Joe Louis Defeated Max Schmeling"
North of Oxford: "We Tell the Sad Stories of Aging Boxers"
Piker Press: "Sugar Ray Robinson"
The Rome Review: "The Practice of Routines in Martin Scorsese's *Raging Bull*"
Scarlet: A Literary Blog: "When The Hurricane Passed: Rubin Carter"
The Spit Bucket Zine: "More Sweet Than Science"
The Sport Literate: "The Phantom Punch" and "Boston Tar Baby"
Tuskegee Review: "The Dilemma of Rooting for Jack Johnson" and "The Life and Resistance of Tom Molineaux"
The Wilderness House Literary Review: "Musings at the Rocky Statue"

"The Phantom Punch" was selected as a finalist in the 2019 Fight Contest Issue of *The Sport Literate*.

Publisher: Leah Huete de Maines
Editor: Christen Kincaid
Cover Art: "Tom Molineaux" by John Young (1755-1825)
Author Photo: Destinee' Allen
Cover Design: Elizabeth Maines McCleavy

Order online: www.finishinglinepress.com
also available on amazon.com

Author inquiries and mail orders:
Finishing Line Press
PO Box 1626
Georgetown, Kentucky 40324
USA

To the sports writers and journalists.

The Lord answered Moses, "Is the Lord's arm too short?
Now you will see whether or not what I say will come true for you."
—Numbers 11:23, New International Version (NIV)

Young man—Young man—Your arm's too short to box with God.
—James Weldon Johnson, "The Prodigal Son"

Float like a butterfly, sting like a bee. Rumble, young man, rumble.
—Muhammad Ali, Activist and Boxer

Contents

The Labors and Toll of Fighting During the Trojan War 1

The Life and Resistance of Tom Molineaux 2

Boston Tar Baby..3

The Dilemma of Rooting for Jack Johnson 4

The Manassas Mauler on the Canvas...5

Bulky Winter Gloves 6

Glimpse of Negro Pride in the Depression (Brown like Samson) 7

More Sweet Than Science..8

The Night Joe Louis Defeated Max Schmeling..9

Sugar Ray Robinson 10

The Practice of Routines in Martin Scorsese's *Raging Bull* 11

I Enjoy Little, Brown Clay 12

The Phantom Punch..13

They'll Be Talking About the Fight of the Century....................................14

The Dichotomy of a Fighter (George Foreman)..15

Debating the Four Kings 16

Ordering Mike Tyson Fights on Pay-Per-View 17

When The Hurricane Passed: Rubin Carter..18

Musings at the Rocky Statue 19

We Tell the Sad Stories of Aging Boxers..20

Notes and References..21

The Labors and Toll of Fighting During the Trojan War

Achilles, dropping his guard and equipment,
Was alone and beside himself inside his tent,
Like a weary fighter abandoned by his guru, posse, and trainers.
There was no reason to celebrate or to swagger around camp,
Despite being the champion and the baddest man alive,
As the Trojan War was on break,
And the Myrmidons were just outside, exchanging body shots,
In tribute to Patroclus, his sparring partner and best friend,
Who did not get up from the long count
When Hector realized he was fighting someone who punched above their weight.
So in this downtime between death and pain, Achilles only spoke to his mother,
The best kind of cornerman to have,
Who sought out Hephaistos to get her fighter back into shape,
And to sew up his physical scars, though she could not quell his emotional ones,
And his need for glory and revenge.
Achilles no longer cared for the corrupt and meddling governing Pantheon,
And how they watched the mortals fight and die for their games.
Now the fight and pain would be for himself, and the sport of it...

The Life and Resistance of Tom Molineaux

Slavery in America had delivered so many death blows,
And was still not yet on the ropes, when Tom Molineaux,
The bare-knuckler from Virginia, came forward,
Before Denmark Vesey, Nat Turner, and John Brown
Fought for the nation's soul,
Before the Missouri Compromise ruptured it,
And before Harriet Tubman made her first crusade up North,
And won the greatest prize; not a belt or title, but freedom.
Boxing is the loneliest sport,
And like the amateur who leaves the old neighborhood for their future,
Tom Molineaux soon leaves the plantation to make the rounds of Europe
Without his sparring mates and kinfolk,
But they understood, and only smiled for the one who escaped,
Before being forced back to their labors on the plantations of Virginia…

Boston Tar Baby

In Boston:
The Land of the 54th Massachusetts,
And Crispus Attucks,
Another brother, Sam Langford, fights;
He's shadowboxing an Invisible Man,
Jabbing at the dark and giving his sparring partner the blackest eyes.

Sam Langford would turn Foreman's face
Into unleavened mush;
He would jack up Dempsey and the Galveston Giant,
Knock down Holmes and Tyson,
Pummel Marciano into submission,
And be the only man who could stop Ali from yappin'.

I don't know about Joe,
But I'm sure the bout would have a noble name:

Brown Bomber vs. Boston Black.

For Sam Langford

The Dilemma of Rooting for Jack Johnson

No one roots for the giants. Not if they're Goliath,
And even more so if they're from Galveston, Texas.
There aren't any black jockeys,
And not many ballplayers either, but at least we got Jack Johnson.
My pop's not too keen on him because he dates white women,
But I just like how he don't care what no one says, and does his own thing;
They even pay him to knock the teeth in of white men;
I want him to win, but the white folks get mad when he do,
And since they can't touch him in the ring, they come after us.
Does the heavyweight title mean so much to him,
Even if they come around to our neighborhoods to burn down the village?
I think it does. It just makes him punch harder, and makes him bolder…

The Manassas Mauler on the Canvas

The painting, and the fight it captures in oil,
Marks the Wild West days of a Wild West game.
It's the 1920s in the Polo Grounds,
And there are rumors that Al Capone might be in attendance,
As he is one, never too far from violence.
The audience, and soon, the artist, George Bellows,
Catch Jack Dempsey being flung from the ring by Luis Firpo,
Despite it looking more like a shove than a punch
If you were to watch the grainy footage.
The painting does not tell the entire arc of these two men,
As the standing Firpo would lose the match,
And the falling Dempsey becomes the icon,
At times, the most famous athlete in Babe Ruth's America.
Fighters falling through the ropes is always an uneasy sight,
The equivalent of a pitcher tripping on the rubber,
But there is humanity in seeing the best of boxers out of rhythm,
As if he was one of us up there, and there is also a moment
To contemplate, as the writers lift him back into the ring;
We're just too close to so much destruction.

Bulky Winter Gloves

Our parents were both the greatest referees and grapplers,
Who set down the guidelines and could dominate the space,
Regardless of distance, and we understood it.
Because of that, the few fights among us boys,
Only took place at those rare pockets of times
When neither was not listening or watching.
The closest we got into the ring was when one parent was working,
And the other was downstairs, fixing dinner in the kitchen,
And we snuck into the plastic tub of winter gear
To grab two pairs of winter gloves, and we went at it,
Ignorant of rules and technique,
Swinging at each like first-fight amateurs
Until one punch connected at the head,
And we immediately put down the gloves, forever,
When my brother and I saw his spittle on my mitt.
I ended my career as the undefeated, mini-flyweight champion…

Glimpse of Negro Pride in the Depression (Brown like Samson)

When he came home from work,
Mule-tired of 5 a.m. starting shifts
And 7 p.m. leaving times,
Pop would abandon all
To light a smoke and
Ear to his favorite radio show.
When it ended, he hummed a tune so often in the air,
That it knew the night
Like the eve knew the moon:

> *Brown like Samson,*
> *Cinnamon and cocoa bean,*
> *Handsome like me.*

During his show,
He would tell us to shush up,
And we gave him peace.
For when it ended, he returned to us,
And lifted us on his shoulders
To march in the street,
Joining everyone we knew
In a Bronze Brigade down avenues
To carry that tune:

> *Brown like Samson,*
> *Cinnamon and cocoa bean,*
> *Handsome like me.*

It was as if they all had ignored
The tired and groan of his bones,
As well as the troubles of his prideful tone,
For Joe Louis had just won.

More Science Than Sweet

After about a week, they go back to the gym
And pound again at the Everlast heavy bag.
Some in their corner want them to continue resting
For a few more days, but it's not like
They were carried away in an ambulance
Or knocked out during their latest loss.
Others want them to stop forever, and while thoughtful,
That's the kind of thinking that shows they never threw a punch.
Unless they're an upcoming-and-comer, they're the ones
Whose names are printed in small font on the title cards.
Their pain goes unmentioned unlike the superstars,
And their names are typically forgotten beyond the ropes
And those who follow the sport.
And still, while often ignored by the mass,
No glory dilutes the love.

The Night Joe Louis Defeated Max Schmeling

When Joe Louis won the Fight of the Century,
And the evening fell like Max Schmeling,
There was a ring shout everywhere in Black America,
And it resonated like the music of hearing John Henry pounding his hammer,
Or Josh Gibson sending a curveball into the atmosphere.

Surging out into the evening, everywhere, were black people,
Like moths from out the Full Moon.

Juneteenth extended long into another day in the heart of Texas.
The jazzmen in Harlem and the bluesmen of Beale Street
Spilled out from their venues to blow and strum their songs,
And Sunday School teachers, way down in Dixie,
Were glad to have made the spectacle a requirement for their students.

After centuries where the occasions
To lift their black arms in celebration had been far too rare,
Joe Louis, some parents' black child, was being cheered by everyone,
And was now not just the strongest man in the world,
But in America, where the black strength of so many had been cut down…

Sugar Ray Robinson

Boxing is not a perfect game of any sort:

The celebrity can be off-putting.
The racism talk, from Johnson-Jefferies
To Mayweather-MacGregor, for marketing, is disgusting.
Seedy promotors and hangers-on
Can take away from the art of it.

And the before and after photos:
Of body jabs, kidney shots,
Swollen heads, and the sour taste of blood,
Is not an easy sight on the eyes,
If they have not already been swelled up.

But this science can indeed be sweet
Whenever he steps into the ring.

The Practice of Routines in Martin Scorsese's *Raging Bull*

When I get to bookstores and events prior to a reading,
I run to the mirror in the bathroom to practice my delivery,
Kinda like the first and last scenes of *Raging Bull*.
Jake LaMotta practices his routines
By reciting Brando's speech in *On the Waterfront*;
I practice by reciting Langston Hughes or *Macbeth*'s "Tomorrow" monologue.
The first man who ever took down Sugar Ray
Has the luxury of his own dressing room.
I just hope someone isn't on the other side of the stall or walks in,
Hearing me talk of nightlife in Harlem and civil wars in Scotland.
That wouldn't necessarily be entertainment for them....

I Enjoy Little, Brown Clay

For the old nation believing them vile,
Uncalled chaos in Miami bubbles
As Louisville Lip and Detroit Red
Laugh and discuss for awhile
The greatness of God, black
And all things untamed
That scar the ranklings
And flame white upset.
And I,
Perusing that photograph
Belonging to unmoved time,
Am just a smile.

The Phantom Punch

The haze of beat-writer cigar fog convened above the canvas.
The strobe lights in the clouds resembled halos in heaven.
The ringside photographers readied their tools to freeze the fighters
Like Greco-Roman artifacts.

And Liston,
Stood over and vanquished by the shuffling, young-man champ,
Listened in a daze to the taunts of new black brashness and rage:
Get up! Get up sucker!

They'll Be Talking About the Fight of the Century Forever

All of the country converged to watch and listen to these two young men,
Caught in the nation's tidal wave of politics and race and divisions, go at it:
Joe Frazier, the plodding slugger out of Philly,
Who could make smoke come out of his gloves,
Against Muhammad Ali, the preening, carnival-barking Muslim
out of Louisville,
Who symbolized revolution and defied the army of America.
And with their gloves and hands as instruments to dispense great cruelties,
They will tickle the world with both their art and pain for 15 beautiful rounds.

And after this, there will be no more nights like these,
Even when they fight again.
The roar and the buzz unfolding round by round in front of the world
Cannot be matched or imitated in sequels, or among other fighters.

Years later, when Frazier is hardened and embittered in his old age,
And Ali has his sharp mind imprisoned by a broken body,
And the world's oldest sport sends out more fighters to its stage,
Bigger and faster and stronger heavyweights from out its corners,
Try as they must, there will never be another bout like this,
A fight that will stand for a century, and many more afterward.

The Dichotomy of a Fighter (George Foreman)

For years, Big George Foreman was the scariest fighter
Since the ol' bear himself, Sonny Liston,
Invoking in the pre-pummeled heads of boxers
On the other side of the ring,
A nervousness that stunted movement and performance,
And a glare and frame that cut deep before the fighting,
And then, just like that, that same scowler
Would soon be smiling in your grandmother's home,
As she pulls out the box for some lean, mean, fat-reducing beef,
As if Big George himself had gotten all of the fight out of him.
It's the war and the treaty within one person…

Debating The Four Kings

In the barbershop scene in *Coming to America*,
If Eddie Murphy and Eddie Murphy and Arsenio Hall and Clint Smith
Wanted to wrangle over a truly endless sports debate,
They would've argued and debated the four kings
Who ruled the sport of boxing in the '80s:
Sugar Ray Leonard, Marvelous Marvin Hagler,
Roberto Duran, or Thomas "Hitman" Hearns;
Filming would've been delayed for hours,
And the release of the comedy classic
Would've been pushed back from June to December…

Ordering Mike Tyson Fights on Pay-Per-View

My pops tells me why he stopped paying to watch Tyson bouts;
He tells the story like how Satchel Paige reminisced on Cool Papa Bell:
So fast, he could flick the light switch and get into bed before it got dark,
Or Vin Scully about Bob Gibson on the mound:
He pitched like he was double-parked.
It wasn't only the biting or the butting or the bruised women
That finally put off my dad;
He got tired of forking over a chunk of paycheck
To see less than six minutes of action,
As Iron Mike ended things before he even got back to his seat with chips.

When The Hurricane Passed: Rubin Carter

Hearing that the Hurricane had passed,
One did not need to have been in the eye of the storm
To know that all things had not been settled.
Out in some prison cell, somewhere,
An innocent man bangs at the wall until his knuckles bleed,
And yells into the ether until he is breathless, and his legs are heavy,
Pleading for one more shot,
In tribute to Rubin Carter…

Musings at the Rocky Statue

It could've been placed outside of a sporting arena;
Before they go off to watch their games,
Rocky would be the last thing the Philly faithful would notice:
They would see him, and their city and their neighborhoods put up on screen,
Overlapping between fiction and reality,
And that famed sculpture of the southpaw going the distance
Sets a mood for athletic excellence that a tailgate simply cannot recreate.
But still, if you've never been to Philly,
The Rocky statue is not outside where the Flyers or Eagles or Phillies play,
But to the steps leading to the city's art museum,
As if the curators and organizers understood,
Beneath the bloodshed and fighting and Hollywood, craft is there…

We Tell the Sad Stories of Aging Boxers

> *Then the man said, "Let me go, for it is daybreak."*
> *But Jacob replied, 'I will not....'*
> —Genesis 32:26, NIV

> *All the people involved in this fight should've been arrested.*
> *This fight was an abomination, a crime.*
> —Ferdie Pacheco, Muhammad Ali's former ring doctor,
> On the Holmes vs. Ali Fight, 1980

They tell now, often in barbershop chairs,
The sad stories and final chapters of aging boxers;
It was the old gladiators sensitive to the grays in their hair
Who will continue the fight, despite the red that trickled down their forehead.

But for the rattling brain and endless headaches,
Slackened jaws that slur the speech,
Sleepless nights, and premature deaths,
The prideful prizefighter will perpetually prowl for one more bout,
And that is when Rocky Marciano swells the faded Brown Bomber's face,
And Larry Holmes pummels an aging Muhammad Ali
In a disgraceful title card, that never should've taken place.

But for one more piece of the action, or for one more paycheck,
Believing this next one shall be the resurrection,
And not just a step closer to early grave,
They will fight, and God help me for paying to watch it all.

Notes and References

In many of the poems in this collection, boxers, and pieces of art, film, literature, and music are referenced and/or were inspirations. Below is a list of notes and references featured and the corresponding poem they are in if they were not clearly stated in the poem. For biographical information, sources include *BoxRec, ESPN, The International Boxing Hall of Fame, Sports Illustrated,* and *The Virginia Museum of History and Culture.*

1. "The Labors and Toll of Fighting During the Trojan War"—The ancient Greek poet, Homer, presents a scene of boxing in his epic poem, *The Illiad*, a text centered on a war between the Greeks and the city of Troy. The scene involving boxing occurs during the funeral games held in honor of Patroclus, the close companion of the Greek hero, Achilles.

2. "The Life and Resistance of Tom Molineaux"—Tom Molineaux was a Virginia slave who fought fellow enslaved people while plantation owners wagered on the fights. Molineaux was granted his freedom after winning one of these contests.

3. "Boston Tar Baby"—Sam Langford, nicknamed "Boston Tar Baby," was an early 20th-century boxer who was reputed to be one of the best fighters of his era, but had difficulty finding opponents due to his skin color. Joe Louis, arguably the greatest heavyweight of all time, was nicknamed, "Brown Bomber."

4. "The Dilemma of Rooting for Jack Johnson"—the history of boxing has featured some of the most creative nicknames in sports. One of these nicknames was attached to Jack Johnson, who was nicknamed "The Galveston Giant," as he was originally from Galveston, Texas. Johnson was the first black world heavyweight champion. Following Johnson's victory against the white boxer James J. Jeffries in 1910, race riots sprang up across the country.

5. "The Manassas Mauler on the Canvas"—George Bellows (1882-1925), painted on canvas, a moment during the 1923 fight between Jack Dempsey and Luis Firpo, when the former was knocked out of the ring. The piece is titled, "Dempsey and Firpo."

6. "Glimpse of Negro Pride in the Depression (Brown like Samson)"—this poem was inspired by Maya Angelou's (1928-2014) eloquent and engaging chapter "Champion of the World" in her autobiography, *I Know Why the Caged Bird Sings*, which discusses a boxing match featuring Joe Louis and Primo Carnera.

7. "More Science Than Sweet"—the sport of boxing has been described as "the sweet science." Journalist, A.J. Liebling's (1904-1963) 1956 collection of essays on boxing titled, *The Sweet Science*, which was an influence on this collection, was named by *Sports Illustrated* as one of the greatest sports books.

8. "The Night Joe Louis Defeated Max Schmeling"—the term "Fight of the Century" has been used to describe several notable fights in the history of boxing, including Louis-Schmeling, Johnson-Jefferies, and Ali-Frazier I, among others. The American Louis and the German Schmeling came to symbolize the philosophical and political differences between the United States of America and Nazi Germany prior to the start of World War II.

9. "Sugar Ray Robinson"—Sugar Ray Robinson, born Walker Smith Jr., was one of the greatest boxers in history, renowned for his exceptional skill, speed, and technique. He held multiple world championships in the welterweight and middleweight divisions during the 1940s and 1950s. His ability in the ring popularized the concept of comparing fighters based on skill rather than size, leading to the phrase "pound-for-pound the best," which became a common way to evaluate and compare boxers. He is widely regarded as the best pound-for-pound boxer of all time.

10. "I Enjoy Little, Brown Clay"—following Muhammad Ali's (then known as Cassius Clay) upset victory against Sonny Liston in Miami to win the heavyweight championship in 1964, he would be joined in the victory celebration by friend and mentor Malcolm X (1925-1965). Malcolm X's birth name before his conversion to Islam was Malcolm Little.

11. "The Phantom Punch"—in arguably the most famous sports photo, taken by Neil Leifer (1942-present) of *Time* Magazine, Muhammad Ali stands over and taunts Sonny Liston in their second fight in 1965. Because match-fixing had occurred throughout the history of boxing, and Liston had fallen down in just the first round of their fight, Ali was yelling for his opponent to get up and continue the fight.

12. "They'll Be Talking About the Fight of the Century"—referring to arguably the most anticipated boxing match and sporting event in American history between Muhammad Ali and Joe Frazier, held on March 8, 1971, at Madison Square Garden in New York City. Both fighters were undefeated heavyweight champions at the time. The fight

lived up to its billing, as Frazier won the match by unanimous decision after 15 rounds in a grueling and closely contested match.

13. "Debating the Four Kings"—the nickname, "Four Kings," refers to the cohort of boxers who were fierce rivals who fought each other throughout the 1980s: ("Sugar") Ray Leonard, Roberto Duran ("Hands of Stone"), Thomas Hearns ("Hitman"), and Marvelous Marvin Hagler; Hagler legally changed his name to Marvelous in reference to his nickname.

14. "Ordering Mike Tyson Fights on Pay-Per-View"—Satchel Paige (1906-1982) and Cool Papa Bell (1903-1991) were Negro League baseball players, renowned for their pitching prowess and agility, respectively. Vin Scully (1927-2022) was the longtime announcer of the Brooklyn/Los Angeles Dodgers, and Bob Gibson (1935-2020) was the pitching ace of the St. Louis Cardinals, who was renowned for his intimidation tactics and pitching velocity.

15. "When The Hurricane Passed: Rubin Carter"—Rubin "Hurricane" Carter was a middleweight boxer whose career was cut short after being wrongfully convicted of murder. Carter's story inspired the 1975 protest song by Bob Dylan (1941-present), "Hurricane," as well as the 1999 film, *The Hurricane*, starring Denzel Washington (1954-present).

16. "We Tell the Sad Stories of Aging Boxers"—in two of the most infamous heavyweight fights, Rocky Marciano easily defeated the former champion and his hero, Joe Louis, in 1951, and in 1980, Larry Holmes defeated his mentor, an aged Muhammad Ali in the 1980 fight, titled "The Last Hurrah."

17. "Musings at the Rocky Statue"—The Rocky statue depicts the fictional boxer Rocky Balboa, portrayed by Sylvester Stallone (1946-present) in the Rocky film series, triumphantly raising his fists in victory. The statue is situated at the base of the steps leading to the Philadelphia Museum of Art.

Thank You

I must first personal thank my Lord and Savior, Jesus Christ, to whom all blessings and guidance derive from in this endeavor.

Thank yous must be extended to my family and friends, with standouts being my parents, Michael and Wynne; your voices and advice continuously flow through me, and thus, this collection and all of my work. I thank my siblings, Jessica, Aaron, and Daniel, as the conversations, the encouragement, the laughter, the fights, and most importantly, and what I am most grateful for, the love, are instilled within these pages.

I must thank again my friend, Justin Vernold, who meticulously combs through my writing and work. Your comments and suggestions are extraordinarily helpful. Your expertise is rare, just as your kindness.

I thank the members of Sundress Publications for allowing me the space and time to edit, revise, and organize this chapbook collection as I served as a Writing Fellow in May 2023.

My thanks goes to the Finishing Line Press Team, and especially editor, Mimi David, for choosing to accept and work on this project with me. Your clarity, feedback, and assistance have been helpful throughout this process.

I am grateful to the writers, Adam Berlin, Leah Maines, and Red Shuttleworth, for taking the time to support this collection; your generosity and time are deeply appreciated.

From the weight-class champions to the up-and-comers still getting used to the speed bag; thank you for the fight.

Matthew Johnson is the author of the poetry collections, *Shadow Folks and Soul Songs* (Kelsay Books) and *Far from New York State* (New York Quarterly Press). His poetry has appeared in *The Maryland Literary Review, Northern New England Review, Roanoke Review, South Florida Poetry Journal, Up the Staircase Quarterly,* and elsewhere.

He is the recipient of nominations for both the Pushcart Prize and Best of the Net awards. He has been selected with recognition from The Hudson Valley Writer's Center, Grand View University, and Sundress Publications. A former sports journalist and editor who wrote for the *USA Today College* and *The Daily Star* (Oneonta, NY), he earned is MA in English at UNC-Greensboro. He is currently the managing editor of *The Portrait of New England* and poetry editor of *The Twin Bill*.

Website: *matthewjohnsonpoetry.com*

www.ingramcontent.com/pod-product-compliance
Lightning Source LLC
Chambersburg PA
CBHW022103080426
42734CB00009B/1472